Hooray for Helium!

Understanding the
2nd Most Common Element

Written by Blake Washington
Illustrated by Mallette Pagano

FERNE PRESS

Hooray for Helium! Understanding the 2nd Most Common Element

Layout and cover design by Kelly Lynn Sexton
Illustrations created by Mallette Pagano
Illustrations created with digital illustrations

Printed in the United States of America

Summary: When Jay asks his sister Kayla why his balloon won't float, he learns how Helium makes a difference in the world.

Library of Congress Cataloging-in-Publication Data
　　Washington, Blake
　　Hooray for Helium!/Blake Washington–First Edition
　　ISBN-13: 978-1-938326-32-5
　　1. Science. 2. Elements. 3. Periodic Table.
　　I. Washington, Blake II. Title
　　Library of Congress Control Number: 2014938551

FERNE PRESS

Ferne Press is an imprint of Nelson Publishing & Marketing
366 Welch Road, Northville, MI 48167
www.nelsonpublishingandmarketing.com
(248) 735-0418

To my niece Kayla, who is wise beyond her years, and to my nephew Jay, who is full of joy and curiosity. Thank you for your love, support, and inspiration.

In just a few hours, my friends will be here.

We'll celebrate my eighth birthday this year.

We'll drink juice, eat cake, and play outside.

My mom even got us a pony to ride!

Before people arrive, we have lots to do.
Cleaning up, getting dressed, and decorating, too!
I run downstairs quickly, excited for the day,
and see some balloons, so I begin to play!

I pick up a balloon and start to blow.

Without much time, it begins to grow.

It gets bigger and bigger until it's just right.

I tie the end, and it's ready for flight.

I throw the balloon up and watch it soar.

But soon it falls down and lands on the floor.

It doesn't stay up in the air very long.

I don't understand this! What could be wrong?

The other balloons are floating high in the air.

But mine is being lazy; it's just not fair!

There must be a reason it won't even try.

I have to ask Kayla and find out why!

"Do you know what's wrong with my balloon?
It started up high but fell down too soon."
"Nothing went wrong. The balloons look the same.
They're just different inside. Let me explain."

"You filled this balloon with your breath, right?
Well, that's not the same for those in flight.

Instead, they have the element helium, Jay!"
"Really? How can you be so sure?" I say.

"I learned about the elements in science class.

They can be solid, liquid, or a gas.

There are more than one hundred and each has a name,

and just like a snowflake,

no two are the same."

The three commonly known states of matter are solid, liquid, and gas. However, there is also a fourth form of matter called plasma. Think of plasma as very hot gas. Fire, lightning, electric sparks, and stars are all examples of plasmas.

"Each element is different, just like you and me."

She picks up her book and says, "Here, look and see.

Elements are on The Periodic Table.

Each has a symbol, like a little label."

"Is that a table where they sit down and eat?"

"No! It shows information, all on one sheet!"

She turns the page and shows me what's there.

Within seconds she finds it and points to a square.

Symbols are usually one or two letters used to abbreviate, or shorten, the element's name. When we read the symbol's name we say each letter so "He" is read as "H-E." This is very helpful when writing chemical compounds and equations. One compound you may already know is water, H_2O. The balanced equation to make water is $2H_2 + O_2 \rightarrow 2H_2O$.

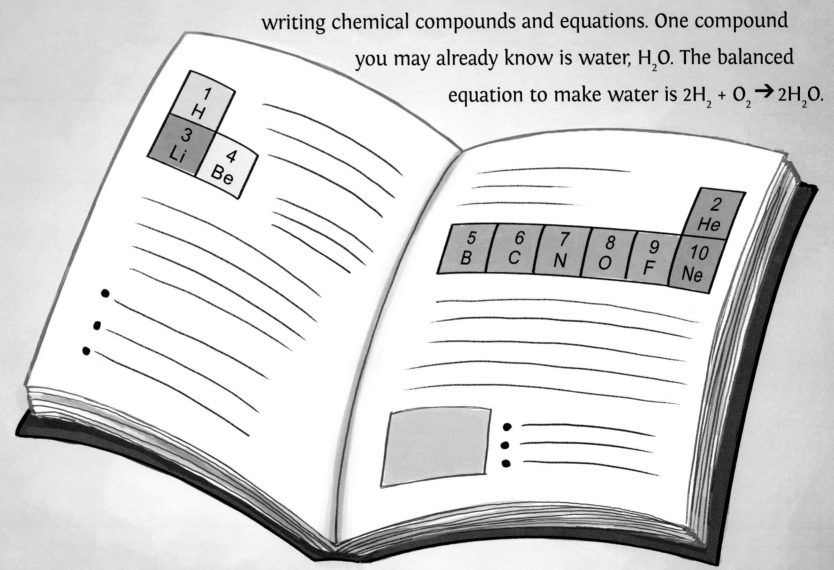

"Here it is, He, atomic number two.

Now, let me show you what helium can do!"

Kayla pokes a hole in the balloon with a pin.

She puts her mouth on it and starts to breathe it in.

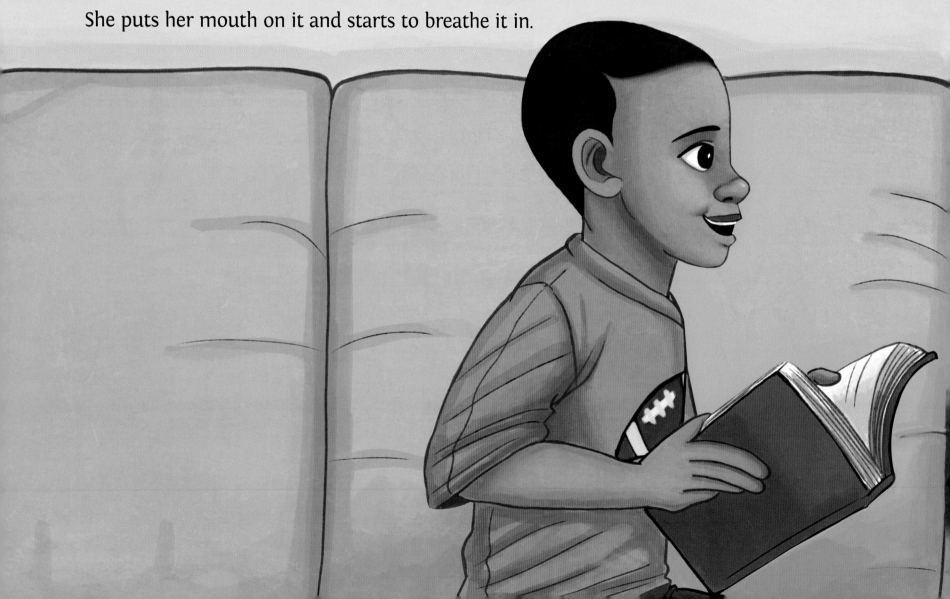

In a squeaky voice she says, "Listen to me now!"

I take a deep breath in and squeak back, "Wow!"

"Helium makes our voices sound strange!

It's less dense than air, which makes it change."

Less Dense

Ping-Pong Ball®

Sponge

Marshmallow

More Dense

Rock

Brick

Marbl

Density is the measurement of the weight of something based on its size. If two objects are the same size but one is heavier, it has higher density. This means the molecules are held closer together than they are in the less-dense item. A rock and Ping-Pong® ball can be the same size, but the ball is less dense than the rock.

"What does less dense mean? I don't understand!"

"It's the same size but lighter than the one in your hand."

"Things less dense will float, and more dense will sink.

Let's go watch your ice float as I pour you a drink."

We go to the kitchen and put ice in my cup.

She pours in some water and the ice rises up.

"Ice floats in water because it's less dense!

The balloons float in air. Now that makes sense."

Try putting a Ping-Pong® ball in a bowl of water. Does it float or sink? If it floats, it is less dense than the water; if it sinks, it is more dense than the water. Experiment with other items like a nickel, sponge, toothpick, crayon, or piece of paper.

"You've learned a bunch, but are you having fun?"

"Of course I am, and it's only begun!

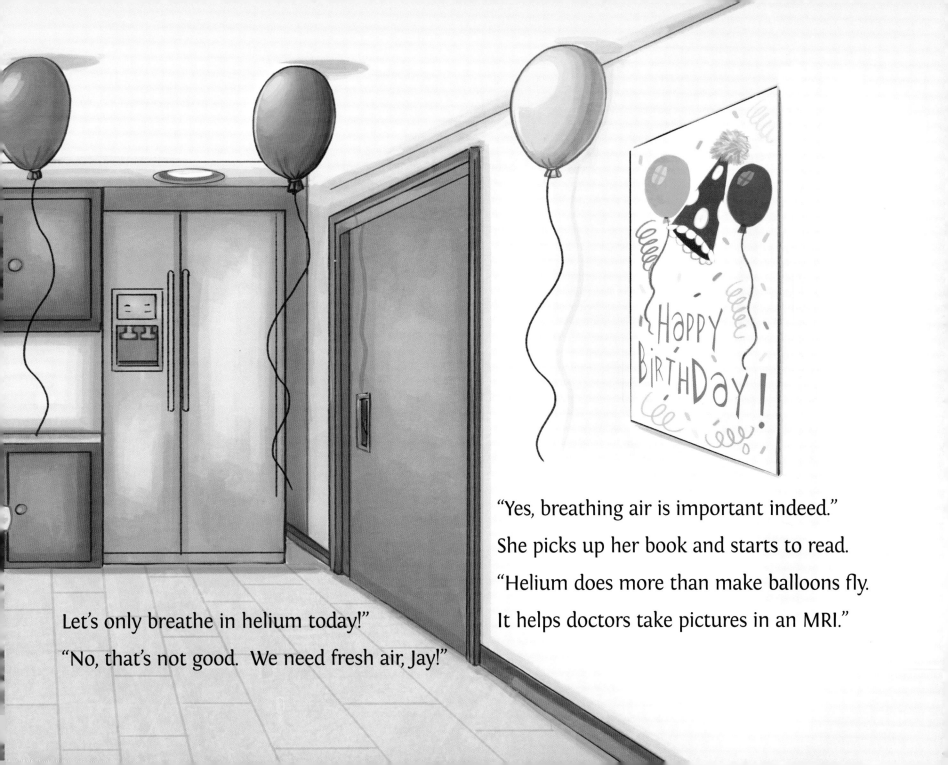

Let's only breathe in helium today!"

"No, that's not good. We need fresh air, Jay!"

"Yes, breathing air is important indeed."

She picks up her book and starts to read.

"Helium does more than make balloons fly.

It helps doctors take pictures in an MRI."

check it out

MRI stands for magnetic resonance imaging and uses strong magnets to create a magnetic field that allows doctors to look inside our bodies. The helium used in MRIs is an extremely cold liquid that helps create more powerful magnetic fields and clear, detailed scans. Who knew helium could be so cool?

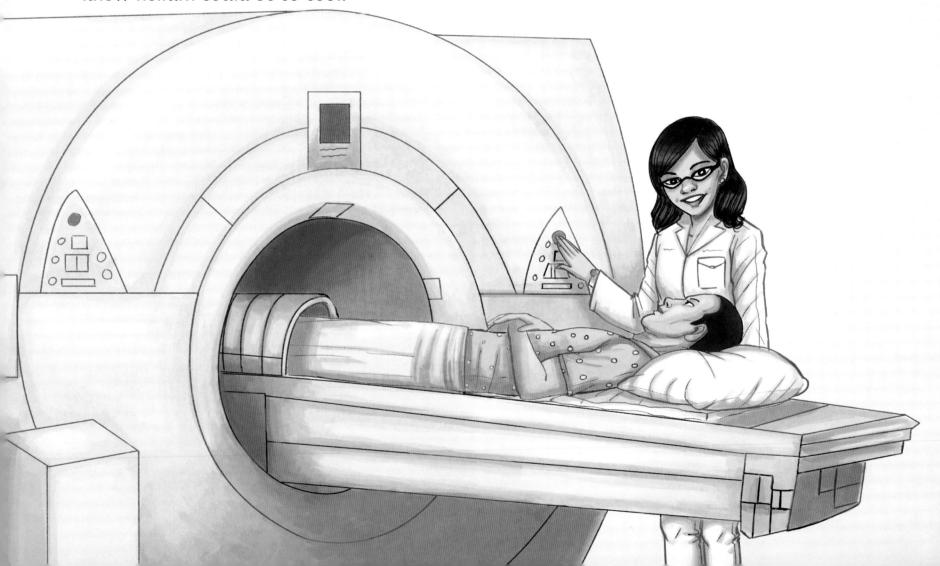

"MRIs can look at muscles, the brain, and the heart."

"Helium isn't just hilarious, it's also smart!"

This element helps make images clear,
and balloons float for my birthday each year.

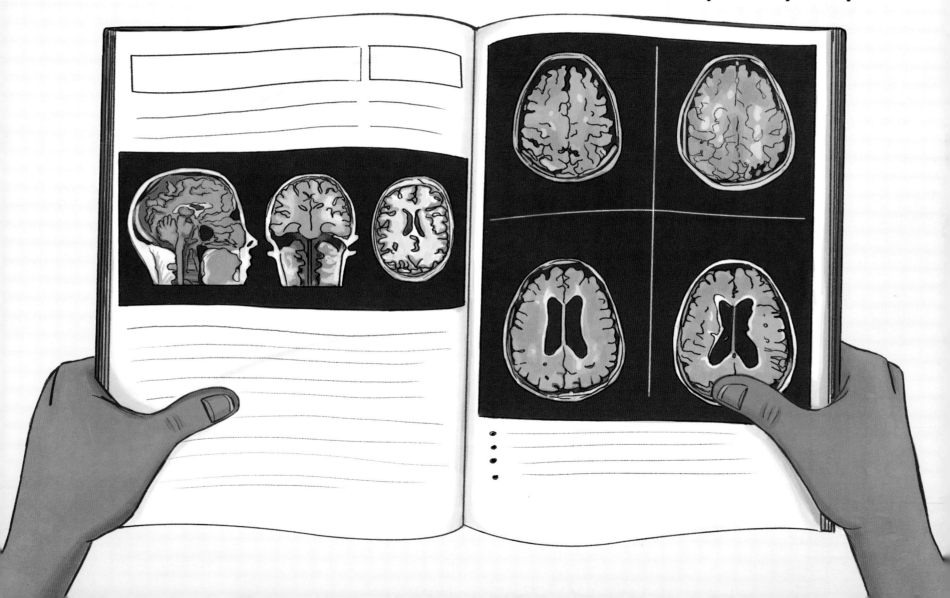

"Are there more elements I see every day?"

"Of course there are. Look around, Jay!"

"This water, this window, this penny, this floor..."

Wow! Elements are everywhere.

I want to learn more!

"There are so many out there, how can I begin?"

"Just explore and ask questions," she says with a grin.

We need to get ready, so she puts down her book.

We've learned a lot, but it's party time—look!

We get dressed, clean up, and decorate.
The balloons are ready. The place looks great.
I couldn't have asked for anything more.
Here come my friends knocking at the door.

Review what you've learned...

What is the name for the list of all of the elements called?

What is helium's symbol?

What is helium's atomic number?

Name two things helium is used in.

Is helium a solid, liquid, gas, or plasma at room temperature?

Which is less dense, a golf ball or a Ping-Pong® ball?

Should you breathe in lots of helium?

Periodic Table of Elements

Key

Atomic # **Symbol** Name	Solid	Liquid	Gas	The State of the Element at Room Temperature (72° F)
		*Synthetic		*Synthetic elements can be made in a science lab but are not found in nature

1																	18
1 **H** Hydrogen	2											13	14	15	16	17	2 **He** Helium
3 **Li** Lithium	4 **Be** Beryllium											5 **B** Boron	6 **C** Carbon	7 **N** Nitrogen	8 **O** Oxygen	9 **F** Fluorine	10 **Ne** Neon
11 **Na** Sodium	12 **Mg** Magnesium	3	4	5	6	7	8	9	10	11	12	13 **Al** Aluminium	14 **Si** Silicon	15 **P** Phosphorus	16 **S** Sulfur	17 **Cl** Chlorine	18 **Ar** Argon
19 **K** Potassium	20 **Ca** Calcium	21 **Sc** Scandium	22 **Ti** Titanium	23 **V** Vanadium	24 **Cr** Chromium	25 **Mn** Manganese	26 **Fe** Iron	27 **Co** Cobalt	28 **Ni** Nickel	29 **Cu** Copper	30 **Zn** Zinc	31 **Ga** Gallium	32 **Ge** Germanium	33 **As** Arsenic	34 **Se** Selenium	35 **Br** Bromine	36 **Kr** Krypton
37 **Rb** Rubidium	38 **Sr** Strontium	39 **Y** Yttrium	40 **Zr** Zirconium	41 **Nb** Niobium	42 **Mo** Molybdenum	43 **Tc** Technetium	44 **Ru** Ruthenium	45 **Rh** Rhodium	46 **Pd** Palladium	47 **Ag** Silver	48 **Cd** Cadmium	49 **In** Indium	50 **Sn** Tin	51 **Sb** Antimony	52 **Te** Tellurium	53 **I** Iodine	54 **Xe** Xenon
55 **Cs** Caesium	56 **Ba** Barium	57-71 **La-Lu**	72 **Hf** Hafnium	73 **Ta** Tantalum	74 **W** Tungsten	75 **Re** Rhenium	76 **Os** Osmium	77 **Ir** Iridium	78 **Pt** Platinum	79 **Au** Gold	80 **Hg** Mercury	81 **Tl** Thallium	82 **Pb** Lead	83 **Bi** Bismuth	84 **Po** Polonium	85 **At** Astatine	86 **Rn** Radon
87 **Fr** Francium	88 **Ra** Radium	89-103 **Ac-Lr**	104 **Rf** Rutherfordium	105 **Db** Dubnium	106 **Sg** Seaborgium	107 **Bh** Bohrium	108 **Hs** Hassium	109 **Mt** Meitnerium	110 **Ds** Darmstadtium	111 **Rg** Roentgenium	112 **Cn** Copernicium	113 **Uut** Ununtrium	114 **Fl** Flerovium	115 **Uup** Ununpentium	116 **Lv** Livermorium	117 **Uus** Ununseptium	118 **Uuo** Ununoctium

57 **La** Lanthanum	58 **Ce** Cerium	59 **Pr** Praseodymium	60 **Nd** Neodymium	61 **Pm** Promethium	62 **Sm** Samarium	63 **Eu** Europium	64 **Gd** Gadolinium	65 **Tb** Terbium	66 **Dy** Dysprosium	67 **Ho** Holmium	68 **Er** Erbium	69 **Tm** Thulium	70 **Yb** Ytterbium	71 **Lu** Lutetium
89 **Ac** Actinium	90 **Th** Thorium	91 **Pa** Protactinium	92 **U** Uranium	93 **Np** Neptunium	94 **Pu** Plutonium	95 **Am** Americium	96 **Cm** Curium	97 **Bk** Berkelium	98 **Cf** Californium	99 **Es** Einsteinium	100 **Fm** Fermium	101 **Md** Mendelevium	102 **No** Nobelium	103 **Lr** Lawrencium

Connect in the Classroom: Blow up a balloon with Carbon Dioxide (CO_2)

Try this fun experiment with normal household ingredients. Before beginning this experiment, make sure you have the supervision of an adult.

What do you think will happen?

Before you begin, make sure you have a hypothesis. A hypothesis is a guess or prediction of what you think will happen. Fill in the blank on this hypothesis or create one of your own.

"If I add baking soda to vinegar in a plastic bottle with a balloon over its mouth, then the balloon will _____ ."

What you'll need:

Balloon
Funnel (use a piece of paper and tape to make a funnel if you don't have one)
4 tsp baking soda

- 1 cup vinegar
- Empty plastic soft drink bottle (16 oz or smaller)

How you'll do it:

Stretch out the balloon to make it easy to inflate.

Pour the vinegar into the bottle.

Using your funnel, add the baking soda directly into the balloon.

Carefully put the stretched balloon over the mouth of the bottle without pouring the baking soda inside the bottle. Make sure there are no holes in the balloon or you will have a big mess!

Lift the balloon up so that the baking soda falls from the balloon into the bottle and mixes with the vinegar.

What's happening?

Write down what you saw after completing the experiment. Did you have any issues? Was your hypothesis correct?
Your balloon should inflate. Adding baking soda to vinegar creates a chemical reaction. The baking soda is a base and vinegar is an acid. When the two combine, they create carbon dioxide (CO_2). The gas rises up and exits the bottle but doesn't escape the balloon, pushing it out and blowing it up.

Mix it up

Now that you've completed this experiment, mix it up! What do you think will happen if you use lemon juice or lime juice instead of vinegar? What would happen if we increased the amount of baking soda? What happens when we change the size of the bottle? Design your own experiment and make sure you have a hypothesis or guess of what you think will happen before you start. Complete your experiment by changing one variable and compare it to the original experiment. A variable is any part of an experiment that can be changed. What variable will you pick to change?

Author

BLAKE WASHINGTON grew up in Strongsville, Ohio, and earned her bachelor's degree in chemical engineering at The Ohio State University. Her passion for science, engineering, and math is apparent both in her career in manufacturing and in the time she spends off the clock tutoring students in disadvantaged school systems. Through her time working with children, Blake noticed a lot of her students demonstrated a knowledge gap in math and science. This was quite the opposite of what she saw in her young niece and nephew, Kayla and Jay. Recognizing Kayla and Jay's extreme curiosity and desire to learn, Blake was motivated to change the direction of her teaching style. She wanted to write engaging children's books that introduced children to math and science topics in an enjoyable way. This is Blake's first book in a series that introduces children to The Periodic Table of Elements and a variety of chemistry concepts. Blake currently lives in Decatur, Georgia, and enjoys spending spare time with friends and family, playing board games, and volunteering at a local homeless shelter. Visit Blake at www.blakewashingtonbooks.com.

Illustrator

MALLETTE PAGANO is a digital artist based in southwest Michigan. She has always loved to draw since she was a little girl. Growing up, her favorite children's books were The Berenstain Bears and the Serendipity series. In 2007, she graduated from Kendall College of Art and Design with a major in graphic design. Since then, Mallette has illustrated several children's books in her career and creates her illustrations in Adobe Photoshop using a Wacom tablet.